DEVELOPING
a
MISSION STATEMENT
for the
MIDDLE LEVEL
SCHOOL

88-1661

National Association of Secondary School Principals
1904 Association Drive • Reston, Virginia 22091

NASSP's Council on Middle Level Education

Alfred A. Arth, *Professor, University of Wyoming*

J. Howard Johnston, *Professor, University of Cincinnati*

John H. Lounsbury, *Editor, the Middle School Journal of the National Middle School Association*

Conrad F. Toepfer, Jr., *Professor, State University of New York, Buffalo*

George E. Melton, *Deputy Executive Director, National Association of Secondary School Principals*

Copyright 1987
National Association of Secondary School Principals
1904 Association Drive
Reston, Virginia 22091
(703) 860-0200
ISBN # 0-88210-204-4

Acknowledgments

The Council on Middle Level Education of the National Association of Secondary School Principals wishes to extend its sincere appreciation to people who participated significantly in the preparation of this document.

Robert St. Clair, president of NASSP, and John Delaney, NASSP board member, gave very valuable and insightful assistance in the original conceptualization and design of this project. St. Clair and Joanne Arhar, assistant principal of Castle Rock (Colo.) Jr. High School, also assisted in the preparation and review of the manuscript and in the review of recommended practices for use in actual school settings.

The council is also grateful to George E. Melton, deputy executive director of NASSP, for giving us our mission and the support to achieve it.

Contents

Preface

A mission statement is a powerful tool for school improvement. Properly constructed, it empowers everyone in the school to assume responsibility for the school's ultimate direction. It is, at once, a commitment, a promise, a guide for decisions, and a set of criteria by which to measure the school's progress toward its defined purposes. Increasingly, the mission statement is indispensible for effective school leadership.

Schools do need to define specific procedures to guide their day-to-day operations. However, procedures are most effective when they respond to the school's defined statement of mission.

This document is designed to help middle level schools begin to develop such a mission statement. Both the process and the active involvement of the school's staff members and clients is essential if the statement is to provide the foundation needed to develop the "nuts and bolts" of effective operational procedures.

DEVELOPING A MISSION STATEMENT FOR THE MIDDLE LEVEL SCHOOL

All effective organizations have a clear sense of their mission. From the largest corporations to the smallest clubs or special interest groups, a clear mission helps members of the organization decide on goals, set priorities, and monitor behavior.

All of the recent literature on organizational effectiveness starts with the premise that without a mission statement that is widely accepted by everyone in the organization, any improvement efforts are doomed from the outset. This involvement of all stakeholders in defining mission has long been a premise of effective collaborative planning.

Middle level schools are less understood than elementary or high schools. Therefore, the mission statement of the middle level school must focus on those educational concerns specific to that level.

Scott Thomson wrote in *Agenda for Excellence at the Middle Level* (1987):

> Schooling is serious business for the young adolescent who must cope simultaneously with a changing self and a changing world. Both need attention or neither will be sufficiently served.

School improvement literature offers the same conclusions. Schools with a clear understanding of their unique missions are more effective than schools that lack a sense of mission. Fortunately, mission statements can be developed and used by schools interested in improving.

Best of all, the negotiation and development of a mission statement is a task that can be directed by the school's leaders. In fact, it is one of the single most important things principals can do to influence the quality of education and the quality of life in their schools.

I. What Is a Mission Statement?

A mission is the special task or purpose established for a person or an institution. In personal terms, it is often referred to as a "calling." For institutions, it is their special reason for existing; it is the thing to which they are most committed. It is the ordering of thoughts that underlie the entire operational practices of the school as an institution.

Effective middle level schools must, as *Agenda for Excellence* states, "understand the relationship of development to learning so that students are not asked to violate the dictates of their development in order to fully participate in the educational program."

A mission is the shared vision of people in an organization about what their ultimate purpose really is. In effective schools, the vision is usually shared among the teachers, administrators, students, and community.

Mission statements are usually short and easily remembered; they are not long, detailed outlines of goals and objectives. Indeed, they may actually be the basis for goals and objectives.

Most importantly, a mission statement is something to which everyone is committed. Without widespread commitment to the mission of the organization, the statement itself is of little use. With commitment, the mission statement becomes a powerful tool in planning, decision making, and evaluating.

Mission statements differ from philosophy statements, goal statements, and lists of specific objectives. The school philosophy tells what the people in the school believe about students, how human beings learn, the role of education in a democratic society, and how education affects the individual receiving it.

A mission statement uses these beliefs to establish an overall purpose for the school.

To illustrate, a philosophical statement might attest to the fundamental worth of the individual:

> We believe that individuals, if given choices, will act for their own benefit and for the common good.

Following from that statement of philosophical belief, then, might come a mission statement such as:

> Park Middle School is committed to cultivating a respect for the individual and encouraging students to make sound, personal choices and decisions.

In other words, this school is committed to letting individuals make significant choices about their own learning and life. That is their mission, their purpose for existing. That is the expectation held for them by the people of Park's community.

Mission statements differ from goal statements because goals set rather specific directions, whereas mission statements establish an overall commitment to a given course. Goals can be viewed as intermediate steps toward achieving the mission. They are incremental achievements that allow us to measure our faithfulness to our overall mission.

The mission statement may be used in setting goals, though. If the mission statement above is translated into goals, they may take the form of institutional goals (to engage students in the school governance process), goals for instructors (to increase the number of choices students are given in selecting learning activities), or goals for students (to develop skills of self-evaluation and life planning).

The mission statement suggests certain goals and gives a screen through which to evaluate the appropriateness of any given goals. But it also allows for the fact that there may be different paths toward that ultimate mission of individual development. The direction is set by the mission, the specific path is established by statements of goals and objectives.

Mission statements also differ substantially from means. Means are the activities, organizational plans, resources, and personnel used to achieve goals.

The mission statement is helpful in selecting means to achieve goals and is especially useful in evaluating school practices to determine if they are consistent with the overall mission of the school. For example, if the mission of the school is to foster individual development, the exclusive use of large group instruction or grading students on a normal curve could be judged as inappropriate.

On the other hand, such a commitment would, presumably, lead to greater use of individualized instruction and criterion-referenced evaluation systems that describe student performance in terms of specific learning outcomes.

II. What Happens in the Absence of a Mission Statement?

Schools that lack a clear sense of mission are characterized by aimlessness and high levels of dissonance. There is little harmony among staff members or between staff members and students. Discipline problems are more likely to occur because staff members lack a common set of expectations, and students have a poor sense of what the purpose of school really is.

A vacuum is created when the school lacks a clear purpose, and other fragmented and contradictory purposes may rush in to fill the void. In such cases, schools may have contradictory rules and policies, teachers may have conflicting expectations, and students may lack a clear sense of what constitutes appropriate behavior.

Students become confused in such an environment, and parents and community members often become frustrated with what they consider to be the inconsistent performance of the school. Scott Thomson observed (1987):

> Unstructured settings can be devastating to morale as well as productivity. Staff members operating in limbo crave a clear definition of expectations, orderly planning, adequate coordination, and feedback about performance. Furthermore, a loose organization will create internal coalitions and conspiracies to fill the power vacuum.

Schools that lack a mission tolerate sometimes bizarre contradictions in programs of instruction. If a math department lacks a clear sense of the school's mission, one teacher may focus on the development of problem-solving skills that are connected to the students' immediate life circumstances. Another teacher may view the math program's primary purpose as sorting and selecting students for advanced study in mathematics at the high school level.

Students in the two classes will have very different experiences, and their parents are likely to be confused (and angered) by the inconsistent expectations, perhaps in the same grade level or even the same subject. In this case, the dilemma is clear, and there is no way to resolve it until everyone in the school agrees upon its fundamental mission for students.

Schools that lack clear missions are often subject to undue influence from external sources as well. If there is no common sense of purpose, the school cannot present a united front to the outside world. Thus, the school or parts of its program are vulnerable to direct influence by groups who see an opportunity to advance their own agenda.

A middle level athletic program that does not have a clear sense of its mission may simply accept a mission dictated by the high school athletic department and function as a selective "farm" system for the high school program. This can ultimately harm the athletic program, because no new talent is cultivated at the middle level; instead, the function is sorting and selecting only.

An English program that does not have a high level of personal literacy as its mission may forego writing assignments in favor of activities that teach students how to respond to low-level standardized test items, or focus on worksheet activities that deal with trivial "basic skills" such as identifying punctuation errors in ways that are unconnected to the students' own writing.

In both cases, the absence of a clear sense of mission permits these less-than-desirable practices to creep into the program. In the first case, the high school dictates the mission; in the second case, the testing program does so. If no mission is established, something will rush to fill the vacuum, and what fills it may be goals that belong to others, and that are not in the best interests of the students.

Mission statements are especially critical for middle level schools. Because of their unique position in the school system, middle level schools are often vulnerable to influence from both the elementary and high schools. The elementary school wants the middle school to continue the program of basic skill development and socialization begun in lower grades; the high school wants the middle school to prepare the students, academically and socially, for the rigors of their program.

In either case, the goals may not be appropriate for the middle grade youngster. But, in the absence of a clear sense of its own purpose, one that is accepted by both the high school and elementary school, the middle level school often finds its purposes dictated by schools that have a stronger sense of their own traditional missions.

Unfortunately, in times past, many people have viewed the mission of the middle level school as to sort and select children for the high school program. In recent decades, the middle level school has accepted other responsibilities that acknowledge the unique nature of the young adolescent, and efforts are made to make the educational program more responsive to those unique needs.

Now, it is especially important that those recognitions be translated into concrete statements of purpose and mission that can guide the middle level school's planning and decision making.

III. How Do You Recognize a Mission Statement?

Certain elements are common to all missions.

A Statement of Purpose

All mission statements address explicitly the overall purpose of the institution or the organization. The purpose of schooling may be to "prepare students for life in the twenty-first century," or "teach students the skills, attitudes, and values necessary for life in the pluralistic society of the United States."

More specialized organizations, such as clubs or service organizations, may have much more specific purposes, such as to "promote the propagation of roses in the Midwest," or "to provide services to the elderly handicapped citizens of Western County."

An Indication of Uniqueness

Mission statements should indicate that the institution's efforts are somehow unique and that the organization is distinguished from other institutions with similar purposes. At the same time, in cases where the mission is truly shared among several institutions or groups, the unique role of the institution should be referenced.

The mission statement of a middle level school should make specific reference to the special population of students served by the school. At the same time, it is helpful to reference the special position of the school in the educational system. To that end, a middle level school's mission statement may include statements such as, "Washington Middle School is committed to preparing young adolescent students with the understandings and skills necessary to cope with their own changes from childhood to adolescence and with the academic skills and knowledge essential for continued school success and life-long learning."

In this case, the school states its own unique mission clearly (to help students cope with the changes they are currently undergoing) and acknowledges its special position in the educational system (to prepare students with skills and knowledge essential for continued school success).

An Explicit Statement of Commitment

All mission statements should be able to pass a "fill in the blank" test. In other words, a reader should be able to fill in the blank in a statement such as, "King Junior High School is committed, above all else, to _____ ." The blank should be filled with the mission of the school, stated as a commitment.

Most important, though, the mission statement should make it clear that the commitment is *shared* among the faculty members, students, parents, and community of the school. Without that sense of shared vision and common purpose, the mission statement is more of a hope than it is a promise.

Thus, mission statements usually acknowledge not only the commitment, but the people who have made it, such as "The community and schools of North County are committed to the maximum development of each individual student's unique abilities and talents." A more limited statement may be, "the students, staff members, and administrators of East Middle School are committed to building respect for and cultivating cultural pluralism in the schools and in the community."

Obviously, all of the groups listed in the mission statement as being committed to the school's mission must have participated in the formulation of the mission in the first place.

A Clear Value Position

A mission statement should be used to help make decisions. Therefore, it must reflect a clear sense of the school's core values, the fundamental values that will guide individual behavior and institutional practices. With the mission statement in hand, anyone should be able to predict what stand a school will take on virtually any curriculum, instruction, or school management issue.

For example, a school that has accepted the mission of "increasing students' respect for and promotion of cultural pluralism" will reflect that commitment in its curriculum. In social studies, simple coverage of events, in chronological order, will give way to a detailed study of the contributions each cultural group has made to American society.

An English program that accepts the mission of "fostering personal literacy" will forego its worksheets for carefully evaluated writing assignments.

First and foremost, the mission statement must be useful in making decisions about whether any given practice is appropriate or not. To do that, it must include a clear value position.

IV. How Does a School Develop Its Mission Statement?

At the outset, it is important to recognize that a school's mission statement must represent a shared vision of the school's purpose. Therefore, the process used to create it must be open, deliberative, and inclusive of all of the school's constituents. This is critical if the mission statement is to guide the behavior of people in the building and be useful as a criterion for assessing the appropriateness of any planned action.

Certain general principles serve to guide the development of a school's mission statement:

☐ *Identify the school's major stakeholder groups and formulate a plan that includes them in the development of the mission statement.* This usually means that the following groups must be included throughout the process: teachers, staff members, administrators, students, parents, community members, representatives from the elementary and high schools, central office personnel, and members of other special groups that are connected in some significant way to the school (such as a business that has a partnership with the school).

☐ *Develop a plan that includes these stakeholder groups in defining the mission statement for your school.* These groups should be involved throughout that process. This does not mean that a standing committee of these people must actually prepare the statement, but that each group is included at each significant stage of the deliberations.

☐ *Use a process that permits the group actually charged with drafting the statement to check frequently with the stakeholder groups to be sure that they are not drifting from the group's understanding of the school's purpose.* Sometimes, committees take on a life of their own, and in making the compromises that committee work demands, the committee members are often unaware how far these compromises may take them from the intentions of the people they actually represent.

☐ *Create a process that focuses on agreements, not disagreements.* Build the mission statement around the points on which agreement is widespread; don't rely on a political (or voting) process to determine the specific points of the school's mission. While total agreement may be impossible, no school wants to have a mission statement that was approved by a one-vote margin. In such cases, the statement will be almost useless in directing schoolwide decision making.

Remember, however, that disagreement is a healthy part of the negotiation process. It is also important that the mission statement take a values stance and that it not be written to accommodate every possible position, no matter how vocally it may be articulated by a single individual or small minority.

☐ *Draft a statement that is short, direct, and easy to remember.* The essential elements of the school's mission statement should be memorable. Everyone in the school should be able to list its principal components without much difficulty. In fact, it is often helpful to post the mission statement, or elements of it, around the school as a reminder to everyone of what the school stands for.

☐ *Once the mission statement is drafted, refer to it frequently and acknowledge its use in decision making.* New practices, policies, rules, activities, or modifications should reference the mission statement. School staff members in particular should make clear, explicit links between the decisions they make and the school's mission statement. The mission statement might even be invoked when certain kinds of assignments are given, as in this example: "Because one of the school's missions is to help you build your problem solving skills, I'm going to give you this problem and let you tackle it without first teaching you the standard method for solving it. See what you can do with your own wits."

☐ *Discuss the mission statement from time to time, and review it on a regular basis to be sure it is still appropriate in view of the population served by the school, changes in curriculum mandates, new community or social expectations, and emerging knowledge about academic subjects and the nature of young adolescent learners.*

☐ *Assure that the mission statement is disseminated widely in the school, the school system, and the community.* It is often helpful if a local newspaper reports not only what the new mission statement is, but the process that was used to develop it. This will increase the amount of confidence the community has in the school, its mission, and its responsiveness to community concerns and priorities.

A Process for Developing a Mission Statement

From these general principles, a fairly specific process for developing a school mission statement can be recommended. The process must be viewed as flexible and adaptable to the school. Just as no school can simply adopt another's mission statement, a school cannot apply a process that does not respond to its unique conditions. This process, then, should be viewed as a general model that invites modifications to fit specific school circumstances.

Step One: Solicit Commitment.

The first step in the process involves seeking commitment from the school community to build a mission statement. A discussion with teachers, parents, student groups, and other constituents about the need for a school mission, its development, and its use in school decision making is essential.

These discussions may be formal or informal, but people need to direct their thinking toward what they believe the special purpose of the school is. Without this "warm up" activity, responses to initial data collection may be given without much forethought and may not represent deeply held convictions.

Step Two: Assemble a Working Group.

The group that will actually draft the mission statement and coordinate its review is assembled. This group should be small enough to be manageable and to meet regularly, and it should be large enough to have some representation from each of the major stakeholder groups.

If a small group is not possible because of the size of the school or the complexity of its organization, a large group might act as a steering committee and include representatives from each constituent group. A smaller sub-group of this larger committee might actually gather data, draft, and evaluate the statement with appropriate guidance from the steering committee.

If the group is to be viewed as truly representative, the criteria by which members are selected should be clear. At a minimum, the writing group should include a parent, a non-parent community member, a school administrator, a district administrator, teachers, students, and a non-certified staff member. The size of the group should probably not exceed 10 members.

Step Three: Gather Data.

This step involves the initial collection of information from constituent groups about their beliefs, values, and purposes for the school. Normally, this information is best collected through a series of interviews conducted by a task force charged with drafting the mission statement. These interviews should include conversations with a large number of students, as many teachers as possible, members of the community, parents, school staff members, representatives from other schools in the district, school board members, and central office personnel.

These interviews should be as open-minded as possible, and the interviewees should be given every opportunity to express their beliefs and opinions about what the school's mission should be.

Lead questions should be used to stimulate the conversation, such as, "What do you think the ultimate purpose of our middle level school should be?" "What is the most important thing for students to leave middle level school with?" "What should the middle level school be doing to really serve the interests of this community?" "In order to be considered successful, what one thing should the middle level school accomplish for its students or this community?"

While it is probably not necessary to tape record these conversations, interviewers should keep accurate notes of the comments made by their subjects. Without these notes, reconstructing exactly what people say will be difficult, if not impossible.

The interviewers must also be careful not to distort the subject's comments. A good rehearsal exercise for interviewers is to have the team divide into pairs. One person in each pair starts by asking the other, "What do you think the mission of _____ Middle School should be?" After listening to the response, the listener must repeat it to the speaker before responding to what the speaker said. The roles are then reversed. This sharpens listening skills and helps prevent the listener from imposing his or her interpretation on speaker's comments.

Step Four: Analyze Preliminary Data.
The task group analyzes the responses to the interviews and sorts statements into Ends (or Mission) or Means (activities or organization plans). This is a critical step, as the group's pur-

pose at this point is to focus on ends, not on operations or activities.

It is often useful to begin this analysis session by listing the beliefs that the interviewees stated to the task group members. This step will assist the group in interpreting subsequent statements about the purpose and mission of the school.

For example, the group may use a category system and list beliefs they heard expressed under each category. A simple category system might include: beliefs about students and student learning; academic subjects and content; community expectations for school; social expectations for school; and the purpose of formal education.

These belief statements will help to formulate mission statements that are consistent with the beliefs held in the school community. All statements of mission should be included, even if some are contradictory. Some statements may be modified to include other, closely related missions and reduce the total number of items on the list to those that truly differ from one another.

The purpose of this activity is to identify the whole range of possible missions for the school, not focus too early on one particularly attractive statement.

Step Five: Create an Instrument To Seek Concensus

The list of mission statements developed above is transformed into a survey instrument that can be used to find major points of agreement among all members of the school's community. The best method for making this conversion is to place a Likert-Scale response with each statement. A sample follows:

	Agree		Undecided		Disagree
1. Raise standard test scores.	5	4	3	2	1
2. Prepare student for high school.	5	4	3	2	1
3. Prepare students for life in a pluralistic society.	5	4	3	2	1

This instrument should be distributed to a large sample of the school's stakeholder groups with the instructions that they mark the number that describes the extent to which they agree or disagree with the school missions stated on the form. The responses should be returned to the task group.

The results of this survey will provide the group with the information it needs to actually draft a mission statement for the school.

An alternative to a Likert-Scale instrument is a cross-impact matrix procedure. In this case, each statement is compared with every other statement and its importance assessed against that of the competing statement. Figure One shows a conceptual model of the cross-impact matrix plan.

Figure One: Cross Impact Matrix

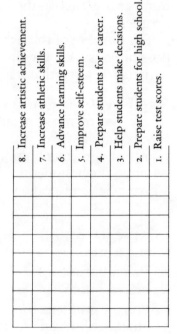

1. Raise test scores.
2. Prepare student for high school.
3. Help students make decisions.
4. Prepare students for a career.
5. Improve self-esteem.
6. Advance student learning skills.
7. Increase athletic skills.
8. Increase artistic achievement.

Each of the statements identified in Step Four is listed in the left-hand column of the matrix. These items are also listed across the top of the matrix, in reverse order. To complete the matrix, statement 1 is compared with all other statements across the row; statement 2 is compared with all of the others; and so on until all statements have been compared with all of the others.

For each comparison, the raters note which of the statements is more important. For example, if the rater thought that statement 1 was more important than statement 10, he or she would put a 1 in the first cell (1, 10).

To develop scores for each statement, simply count the number of times it was chosen. The greater the number of times it was selected, the more important it is in comparison with other statements of mission.

Step Six: Draft the Mission Statement.

The task group reviews the results of the survey and uses that information to draft the mission statement. First, the group must analyze the survey results to identify the mission statements on which there is *universal or near-universal agreement*. This is essential if the mission statement is to be accepted by the stakeholder groups in the school. If a significant portion of the group does not accept a statement, its members will not use it as a guide for their own behavior.

The number of statements on which there is universal agreement is likely to be small, making a mission statement quite short, as opposed to a comprehensive listing of expectations that will offer concrete direction for every school endeavor. It will be a general statement of direction and commitment that must be interpreted in its application to specific school situations.

The second stage of this step requires that the task group actually draft a mission statement that responds to the survey information and that includes the parts outlined in Chapter III.

Step Seven: Solicit Agreement on the Statement.

This is one of the most important stages in the process, and one that can be time-consuming and deliberative. This step has several sub-steps that must be completed if the process is to be effective.

□ *Presenting the Statement.* If the task group has a steering committee, the group should make the first presentation to that committee, soliciting recommendations for modification while insisting that the group remain faithful to the data gathered from the interviews and in the survey.

After this presentation, the statement should be presented, in whatever form feasible, to the other stakeholder groups. This may include meetings of intact groups (i.e., teachers, staff members, administrators, parent council, student council, etc.), mailings or distributions to other, less well-defined groups (parents, community leaders, business partners), and direct distribution to students (perhaps in classes, during which time the statement is discussed).

□ *Exploring Implications.* The task group must help other stakeholders understand the consequences of the mission statement. It would be helpful for them to present hypothetical situations (should students be "cut" from an athletic team; should choral participation be based on auditions, etc.) and show what decisions would probably be made if the mission statement were actually guiding behavior. If possible, sample scenarios should be created for each stakeholder group.

□ *Encouraging Reflective Consideration.* The task group should encourage members of the stakeholder groups to consider the implications of the mission statement for them. They should be asked to have the statement placed on the agenda for the group's meetings (i.e., student council, academic departments, teams, administrative council, parent council, etc.) or discussed, informally, with at least two or three other members of each stakeholder group.

Groups should be asked to endorse the statement or make modifications necessary for them to endorse it. These endorsements and modifications should be returned to the task group.

Step Eight: Prepare a Final Draft.

Using the endorsements and modifications recommended by stakeholder groups, the task group drafts a final version of the mission statement that accommodates as many of the recommendations as possible. In cases where an accommodation cannot be made, the task group is obligated to explain to the individual recommending the modification why it cannot be made in the final version. In addition to showing courtesy, this provides an opportunity for the task group to solicit support from individuals whose idiosyncratic interests cannot be accommodated.

Step Nine: Disseminate the Final Draft.

Once the final draft has been prepared, it should be disseminated as widely as possible. Copies should be mailed to parents and distributed to students, school staff members, and teachers. If possible, a copy of the statement should appear in the local newspaper, and copies should be mailed to major civic organizations with the request that it be distributed to members.

An integral part of this process also requires that the implications of the statement be widely discussed. A faculty meeting should be devoted to the topic, as should a student council meeting or even a schoolwide assembly. The principal objective of these discussions is to familiarize people with the statement and illustrate how it should be used in making decisions about programs, policies, and individual behavior.

Special schoolwide modifications resulting from the new mission statement should be recommended and discussed.

Step Ten: Assess Impact and Review the Statement.
On a regular basis, the impact of the statement on the school's operation should be assessed. At the same time, the statement itself should be reviewed and reaffirmed. If modifications seem warranted, they should be undertaken, but the procedure for modifying the mission statement should replicate, as nearly as possible, the process that created it.

Perhaps the most important questions to answer in this impact assessment are:

- Has the statement affected school practices and individual behavior?
- Has the effect of the statement been good?
- Is the statement being interpreted as intended?
- What unforseen events emerged because of this statement?

It is also important that this assessment be conducted on a routine basis. If not, the statement will lose its vitality and become yet another document that no one pays much attention to in daily operations.

V. How Do You Use a Mission Statement?

There isn't much point in spending the time and effort it takes to develop a mission statement if it isn't going to be useful in the operation of the school. In fact, the mission statement can be the most powerful management tool at the school administrator's disposal.

If the statement is truly representative of the shared vision of what people expect the school to do, it empowers the principal and the rest of the professional staff to take actions that advance the school's mission. To the extent that the actions taken clearly advance the mission of the school, the administration (or teachers) can expect a high degree of agreement with those actions.

Beyond the general contribution a mission statement makes to the management of the school, it can also be useful in more specific ways:

To Review Programs, Policies, and Practices

The purpose of this review is to determine whether or not these elements of the school conform with the schools avowed mission, and to identify elements that advance the school's mission or impede it.

If, for example, a school's mission statement includes "to prepare students for life in a technological society," the program should obviously make use of technology in every possible subject area and in every possible way. In addition, the mission statement suggests that some formal study of technology—its uses, misuses, ethics, costs—should also be included in the program of the school.

In a school that pledges "to equip students for participation in a democratic society," we would expect, as a matter of policy, to find an active student government with some real (if limited) decision-making authority, and a concerted effort on the part of the school administration to encourage student participation in school governance.

A school that accepts as its mission, "to provide instruction that matches the developmental needs of young adolescents," would display instructional practices that are active, inquiry based, and heavily oriented toward cooperative learning. There would be a few prolonged lectures and little reliance on seatwork.

In short, the mission statement permits school personnel to determine if what they are doing coincides with what they value and what they accept as their special purpose for existing as a separate educational unit. It is a way of deciding if what they do is consistent with what they believe.

To Make Daily Decisions

In many ways, the mission statement is most useful as a guide for everyday behavior of students, staff members, teachers, and administrators. It should direct the kind of instructional decisions teachers make, the kinds of management decisions principals make, the kinds of support-services decisions staff members make, and the behavioral decisions students make.

If a school accepts as its mission "to cultivate a respect for diversity and the rights of the individual," we would expect to find a high degree of individualized/differentiated instruction in classrooms; administrative tolerance for the expression of unpopular opinions, provided they are not harmful to the orderly operation of the learning process; highly individualized counseling and academic schedule planning; and student relations in which there is little peer criticism and a high degree of self-monitoring.

Most important, the mission statement equips all members of the school community (indeed, it empowers them) with standards by which to judge not only their own behavior but that of others. In that sense, the entire school community sets limits on what is acceptable behavior, and all members of the community are equally able (in fact, obligated) to share in the maintenance of those behavioral standards. The vacuum that permits so much dissonance has been filled by a common sense of purpose that is represented by the mission statement.

To Set Goals and Priorities

With a mission clearly articulated, it is relatively simple to set goals and priorities for the school. If the mission statement includes, "to prepare students to solve problems and make sound decisions about their own lives," the school must answer two questions: What are we doing now to facilitate that mission? What should we be doing to advance that mission?

The answer to the first question comes from the program review activity outlined above, the answer to the second is, in fact, a statement of goals and priorities for the school.

The same is true for each aspect of the school's program as well.

Staff members in each program area (including academics, exploratory courses, cocurricular areas, etc.) should review their programs in light of the mission statement and set goals for themselves and their programs. Once established, these goals can be placed on a timeline in priority order and, in fact, yield a long-range plan for the development of the school and its constituent parts.

To Reward and Reinforce People in the School

A mission statement is closely connected to the reward and incentive system in the school. Not only does the mission statement allow the school to identify the kind of performance it wants to reward and reinforce, the reward system itself will strengthen the mission statement by calling attention to people who act in ways that the mission statement encourages. People who are rewarded provide visible models to the rest of the school of just what it means to "act out" the school's mission.

Because of this close connection, it is crucial that the reward system be consciously and consistently linked to the mission. When distributing rewards it must be made clear that the reward is for advancing the mission of the school. The specific performance that led to the reward must also be identified, or people may believe the reward is given for a performance that does not necessarily support the school's mission.

If a school's mission calls for the "cultivation of social responsibility," it is appropriate to give rewards for that kind of activity. If the school's star athlete is given a "good citizen" award for advancing the school's mission by volunteering at a retirement home, it must be made clear that the reward is for the service, not for athletic achievement.

Unless that distinction is made clear, other students may feel that the reward was yet another recognition of the star's overall prowess and popularity, and decide that they will never be eligible for such a reward because they lack the necessary prerequisites. Such an attitude will quickly scuttle a school's devotion to its mission.

VI. What Else Will a Mission Statement Do for the School?

Beyond the outcomes discussed above, other significant things may happen in the school that creates a strong sense of mission. Some of these things are likely to be unfamiliar and, at first, just a bit uncomfortable. But, from an organizational health point of view, virtually all of them will strengthen the school and its performance. They will also become not only comfortable, but normal routines of school life.

First, the publication of a mission statement equips everyone in the school and in the community with criteria by which to judge the school and its performance. If the mission is truly a statement of what the school is committed to, it is also an agreement to be held accountable for working toward that mission.

The advantage of this set of circumstances is clear: the school has provided the criteria by which to judge its own effectiveness. This reduces the likelihood that the school will be judged, within the school system or by the community, on idiosyncratic or suddenly shifting criteria. It reduces evaluative paranoia and allows the staff members to focus on major goals and objectives, not brushfires set by school critics.

Second, just as the mission gives a set of criteria by which to judge a school, it also gives a set of criteria by which to judge the behavior of everyone in the system. While this is desirable, it is also potentially threatening to those who are not accustomed to being held accountable for their behavior.

To some extent, the presentation of criteria automatically invites evaluation, and, with the publication of a mission statement, there is likely to be more interest in judging the performance of professional staff members, in evaluating and intervening in student behavior, and in assessing the performance of school administrators in advancing the school's mission.

Again, this speaks of organizational health. The criteria are clear, everyone has agreed upon the mission and everyone in the system is responsible for monitoring compliance with the mission. Presumably, everyone who participated in the development and ultimate acceptance of the mission statement is also eligible to participate in this continuous monitoring and evaluation.

Finally, the presence of a clear sense of mission argues for more consistency of behavior in the school—consistency among teachers, between teachers and administrators, among the support personnel, and among students. Because a mission statement outlines the ultimate purposes of the school, it avoids specifying detailed processes for achieving these purposes. This increases the tolerance for multiple ways of doing things and argues against the rigid application of specific rules of procedure.

At the same time, however, schools with strong mission statements are (and should be) intolerant of behavior or practices that run contrary to the school's mission. If everyone agrees where the school is going, there should be little need to argue about the specific methods for getting there. Discussion should be saved for identifying and eliminating practices that are clearly at cross purposes with the mission of the school.

The mission is designed to reduce unproductive dissonance. But what happens if one person or a small group of people (teachers, students, administrators, or parents) seek to undermine the school's mission? Provided an orderly mechanism exists for the review and modifications of the school's mission, the options available to respond to unproductive dissonance are the same as those used in society at large.

As individuals, we aren't able to select the laws we are going to obey or the social norms we are going to follow. If we elect to ignore the laws and norms established by our fellow citizens, we do so with the expectation that we will face certain consequences. In other organizations, the same principle holds true, and the control mechanisms are similar.

First, we usually experience strong peer pressure to accept the norm. If that fails, certain sanctions are applied, such as withdrawal of rewards or the application of specific punishments. If those fail, the individual is usually isolated so that he or she cannot damage the rest of the system. Ultimately, the person may be removed from the system entirely.

If individuals will not support the universally agreed-upon mission of the school, and peer pressure or official sanctions are unsuccessful in changing that decision, the school should be empowered to isolate the individual to minimize his or her effects on the rest of the system or to remove the person from the system altogether.

VII. Conclusion

Like people, institutions need a sense of purpose and direction to be effective. That sense of mission must be important and capable of withstanding careful scrutiny. To assure that the mission statement is both important and durable, the process that creates the statement must be broadly based, open, and deliberative. An effective school will have a clear, widely-accepted statement of its mission and will have a powerful tool to use in school improvement efforts.

References

NASSP Council on Middle Level Education. *An Agenda for Excellence at the Middle Level*. Reston, Va.: NASSP, 1985.

Thomson, Scott D. "Leadership and Power," *NASSP News-Leader*, January 1987.

Sample
Mission Statement

The faculty, staff, students, and community of Parkside Junior High School are devoted to academic excellence and the cultivation of individual strengths and talents in a supportive environment where individual differences and respect for the rights of others guide school and community behavior.